Be
Victorious!

Lessons from World War I
for Business
and
Everyday Life.

Dedication.

This book is dedicated to my grandfather,

William Arthur Edward Murray MM,

(1883 – 1956)

Sergeant in the Royal Garrison Artillery

during the Great War.

One of the lucky ones who came home.

CONTENTS

"You can never plan the future by the past."
Edmund Burke.

INTRODUCTION

Do you keep getting defeated in business, at work or at home? This book draws lessons from the First World War that apply to most of our lives. Is now a good time to turn things around?

On the eleventh of November 2018, we are commemorating the hundredth anniversary of the end of the First World War. Over the last few years, we have heard a lot about that conflict: the causes, the major battles and, especially, the impact on the lives of people at home as well as at the Front.

It has been said, however, that the main use for the past is for us to learn from it, and even if you don't take much interest in history, there are lots of lessons to be learnt from the Great War, and not just for soldiers or politicians. It was a classic case of How Not To Do... lots of things, as well as containing the odd exceptional example that may be worth copying!

This book shows how to apply some of the lessons of that War to management. But management can't be separated from other aspects of life, so there will be something for you in this book.

"I will not advise His Majesty to declare war while peace may yet be had!"

Sir Robert Walpole, Britain's first Prime Minister, speaking in 1739.

CHAPTER I

Could Some Risk Management Have Prevented World War I?

Although people still argue about the causes of the Great War and ask who was to blame, it seems clear that nobody in the British Government actually wanted a war. Well, it seems some of them may have done, but only when it got to the point that the alternatives looked to them to be unacceptable.

It seems that the Russians and the French were also reluctant participants. Even the Kaiser does not seem to have wanted what he got. So what went so very wrong? Let us look at it from a Risk Management point of view.

If war was an outcome they all wanted to avoid, what risk control measures did they put in place to prevent it?

- The most important of these was diplomacy, and that meant alliances. The idea was that every country had allies and that they would all protect each other, so that nobody would be foolish enough to attack anyone else. The disadvantage of this approach was that there was no mechanism for preventing a conflict from escalating. Any local dispute was likely to end up going global. As it did.

- The second risk control measure was deterrence. It was thought that having a large army would deter other countries from attacking. Since all the major powers followed this approach, however, it only added to the risk that any conflict would be really serious. (Strange as it may seem, Britain, with a huge worldwide Empire, had the smallest army of all the major powers, possibly because people trusted in the Navy and in diplomacy).

- The other risk control measure lay in the belief that the leaders of the various nations knew and understood each other, so knew how far to go. It was rather like a game of poker. In the 19th Century the German leader Otto von Bismarck had been famous for his ability at brinkmanship. Unlike him, sadly, Kaiser Wilhelm II forgot to stay on the right side of the brink, as he seriously misjudged the British in particular.

We all know that diplomacy and deterrence failed in 1914 with catastrophic results. In short, none of the above measures succeeded in preventing the War, and it could be argued that they increased the risk.

What else could have been done? It might have helped if there had been an institution such as the United Nations to allow issues to be settled at the conference table before they got to the battlefield.

Do you have any risk control measures which make the risks worse? Do you need to review them?

"A zebra never changes its spots!"

Al Gore.

CHAPTER II

So You Think You Know Who Your Friends Are?

Some years ago I accidentally came upon something which I found both sad and ironic, giving me cause to rethink my understanding of some of the supposed certainties of life.

A British Officer's Legacy.

I knew that my father-in-law had fought in the Second World War until he was wounded and captured at the Battle of Monte Casino, after which he was held as a prisoner of war until he was liberated upon the allied victory. Then he became part of the Army of Occupation in Germany where he witnessed the desperate poverty of most of the population following the collapse of the economy of that country. He observed many Germans having to exchange all sorts of possessions not only for relative luxuries like cigarettes and chocolate, but also for basic necessities such as bread, soap or tea. He himself accumulated a collection of objects he had accepted in exchange for whatever he could spare from his own rations. Among these were some former belongings of an old man whom he had known, who had been a gardener at a British base near Hamburg at that time.

When my father-in-law died in 1988, my wife and I came upon a small metal box in which he had kept some of the more interesting of these items, mainly coins and medals. Among these was a medallion inscribed: *"II Hannover 1813 – 1913"*. I know nothing about it, but assume its former owner had served in the 2nd Hanover Regiment and had been given this in 1913 in its centenary commemorations.

Whose Side Were They On?

I was struck by the enormous irony of this. In 1813 Germany was a geographical rather than a political entity and Hanover was an independent state, including Brunswick and Bremen as well as the City of Hanover itself and of course much of the surrounding countryside.

The ruler of Hanover in 1813 was the British King George III. Therefore the Hanoverian Army fought alongside the British against Napoleon's forces and played an important role in the allied victory at the Battle of Waterloo in 1815 under the command of the Duke of Wellington. Throughout the rest of the Nineteenth Century, Hanover remained a friend of Britain until her incorporation into the German Empire in 1870 – a move not altogether welcomed by the majority of its citizens. Indeed, it is thought that support for the ambitions of the Kaiser was particularly low in Hanover, especially when war with Britain became imminent. Similarly, in the 1930's Naziism was less popular in Hanover than in most parts of Germany.

Be Prepared For Change!

In 1813 when the 2nd Hanoverian Regiment was formed, nobody would have imagined that it would be called upon to fight against Britain a century later. Even in 1913 the idea would probably have seemed incredible. However, a lot can change in a century, or even in a year. Life has its surprises.

Even in our present age, when there are so many developments in technology every year, when the economic climate is far from static, it is easy to assume that most things do not change very much. It is easy to suppose that once a decision has been made, if it was the right decision at the time, it can stand unchallenged for ever. It is easy to think that relationships remain constant, that customers will stay loyal, that doors once closed to your business will remain closed. It is, in short, easy to be wrong.

Change? Here?

Many people who agree with the above, will be surprised to find how many things in their business or in other areas of life are the way they are because they always have been. Perhaps an idea that was rejected before will seem more acceptable now.   Perhaps a company that would not do business with you before has gone through some changes and will be more receptive now. Perhaps something that was too expensive before may have become more affordable now. Perhaps a risk is now much greater or much less than when last reviewed. Perhaps a risk control measure is no longer as appropriate as it was.

What have you not reviewed lately? What has always been unthinkable? What do you now need to think about?

"Example is the school of mankind and they will learn at no other."

Edmund Burke.

CHAPTER III

Learn Your Lessons

One of the most depressing things any study of the First World War will reveal is that almost all the countries involved persisted in repeating the same mistakes over and over again. (A practice which Albert Einstein defined, in another context, as evidence of madness). Here are just a few of the more obvious examples.

- The French kept sending their cavalry to charge against machine-guns and rapid-firing rifles, with the same result, time after time, until they had hardly any cavalry left. This was, fortunately, one mistake the British and Germans avoided.
- The British, and most others, persisted in preceding every major infantry push with a heavy artillery bombardment. This invariably failed to do very much damage to the enemy, but made the ground all the more difficult to cross, making the infantrymen easier targets for enemy guns.
- The overall approach of fighting in trenches and periodically trying to advance slowly in large numbers on foot, directly towards the enemy, was repeatedly unsuccessful. Winston Churchill called this "sending men to chew barbed wire".

- Alternative tactics were almost always rejected. The introduction of tanks was resisted for a long time.

So one of the first lessons from the First World War is to learn your lessons!

Of course we all know the old saying: "if at first you don't succeed, try, try again". However, it should probably be interpreted as "try again, having learned the lessons of past failures". *What mistakes are you constantly repeating in your business, or in any part of your life? Would today be a good day to stop and think?*

"*I don't know what effect these men will have upon the enemy, but, by God, they terrify me!*"

The Duke of Wellington.

CHAPTER IV

Trust

As I have said in the last chapter, one of the criticisms made about the leaders on all sides during the First World War was their apparent failure to learn from their mistakes. Once both sides had established their positions in the trenches, the tactics hardly ever changed despite the stalemate. Winston Churchill commented at the time that there must be an alternative to "sending men to chew barbed wire." Yet no such alternative seems to have been adopted until towards the end of the War when the use of tanks was introduced.

Confessions of a General?

You might think this was the result of a lack of imagination on the part of those in charge, and to some extent you could be right. However, I learnt recently of another factor influencing their decisions, or arguably their lack of them. This was revealed by Field Martial Haigh in his memoirs. He explained that he would have considered trying different approaches if the Army had consisted of professional soldiers. Being aware that the vast majority of the men were volunteers, and later conscripts, with only a limited amount of basic training, Haigh, and apparently the other generals, did not trust them to carry out any more complicated tasks than those required for returning enemy fire from the trenches and occasionally attempting to advance in great numbers straight towards the enemy, through bomb-craters and over barbed wire, while being fired upon. Haigh wrote that he was afraid we could lose the War if he allowed the men to try anything more difficult, and it had gone wrong.

You might think that this lack of trust in the men was due to the snobbish attitude prevalent at the time among the upper classes, of which he was a member. Many of them seemed to think uneducated people were unintelligent. They also believed, with perhaps more justification, even if they may have been actually wrong, that people whose lives were spent doing what other people told them, would not develop the initiative needed to carry out difficult tasks unsupervised, and that on the battlefield, quick-thinking is essential if there is any chance of encountering the unexpected. It has to be said that the horrors experienced day after day at the Front probably did not contain anything unexpected after a short time.

You might however adjust your opinion, as I tell you that the Field Martial extended his lack of trust to the officers as well as other ranks. He believed that even these Eton-and-Oxbridge-educated sons of the aristocracy had such little knowledge or experience of military things that they were quite likely to make very poor decisions if they were given too much responsibility, with possibly catastrophic results.

How Trusting are You?

Whether Haigh was right or wrong in his assessment of the men and the officers under his command, I certainly believe that trust is an essential element in battle. I am pleased to tell you that I have come to this understanding at second-hand, but am convinced it is true. It is also true that we need trust if we are to work together effectively in many other areas of life, and it is worth asking yourself how much you trust the employees, partners or other colleagues in your business. Perhaps you are, like me, not of a naturally trusting nature. Perhaps you have had good reason to regret trusting people too much in the past. Perhaps you are reluctant to delegate. Do you believe that *"if you want something doing right you have got to do it yourself"*?

The Alternative?

When I look back, or look around, I can think of too many examples of managers who did not or do not trust their subordinates. In many cases the remedy would be better training or mentoring, not to mention communication. Remember, we have to develop the managers of the future. In most businesses it should be possible to organise things so that one slip-up by an employee would not be catastrophic. An option not available to Field Martial Haigh.

If you really cannot trust the people around you – if you are sure the answer does not lie in training etc. – then perhaps you should think of changing something. Like your employees, or yourself.

"Someone had blundered."

Alfred Lord Tennyson,

The Charge of The Light Brigade.

CHAPTER V

When Things Go Wrong, What Do You Do?

Some people say you should never prepare for failure as it creates the wrong mindset, but there is a risk of becoming so focussed on your plans and targets that you do not know how to react if things do not go the way you had hoped. This chapter looks at some of the ways people reacted to the failures and frustrations of the First World War, and considers what lessons we can apply to the setbacks we may experience in business and other areas of life.

Rudyard Kipling wrote in the poem If: "... if you can meet with Triumph and Disaster, and treat those two imposters both the same," to remind us that we have to avoid overreacting to either success or failure in life. Many people still need to learn this lesson, and in this chapter we will be concentrating on how to cope with failure, and especially how **not** to react to it, drawing on many examples of how leaders, the press and the public reacted at various times to the almost incessant bad news from the Front during the First World War.

41

In response to the continuing stalemate on the Western Front, the mistake most frequently made was to look for scapegoats. Many were found. Mostly, blaming them, apart from being unfair, did nothing to help win the war.

1. **Cowards.** From an early stage, before conscription was introduced, there was a lot of hostility to any young men who did not join the armed forces. They were considered cowards and often given white feathers. Yet some men were more useful in their civilian occupations, others were physically or mentally unsuitable for armed service.

2. **Deserters**. Similarly, men who could not cope with the stress of battle and ran away were shot for cowardice or desertion.

3. **Conchies**. Later, when conscription was introduced, with much controversy, conscientious objectors were treated very badly by the Courts and the public.

4. **Spies** were (probably wrongly) regarded as a great threat and many foreigners, and even British people with sometimes quite slim connections with Germany, were often treated with suspicion and hostility, even if not actually arrested or charged with anything.

5. **Winston Churchill**, First Lord of the Admiralty, was blamed for the failure of the

Dardanelles campaign in 1915 where a lot of lives were lost to no benefit. The irony was that he was trying harder than anyone to find a way of either ending the war or at least moving it away from the trenches. He kept proposing more imaginative approaches, including the use of tanks and aircraft. If the Dardanelles campaign had succeeded he would have been <u>very</u> popular.

Two groups of people were blamed with some justification: **hoarders and profiteers**. The food shortages in 1917 were so serious that hoarders were putting other people's lives at risk. Profiteers, whilst not directly affecting the war effort, made the sacrifices of the majority seem all the harder to bear, so damaging morale.

What relevance has this for us?

I can recall all too well stories where victims of major disasters have been blamed, or where people whose failings could be counted as only minor contributions were made into scapegoats. I expect you could think of similar but less publicised things where you work. In my work, dealing with liability claims, I have often found it difficult to convey reality to the people I have been trying to help: they have been reluctant to accept their own share of the responsibility for an accident to themselves or to someone else.

The Pity.

The sad thing is that turning the blame on the wrong culprits, whether in business, in war, or in any aspect of life, leads to a failure to see what was really wrong and how to do better in future. The same was true during the Great War when too much effort went into fighting the wrong enemy, and too little into discovering the causes of the failure to break the stalemate and find new strategies.

I have often heard it said that failure is one step towards success. It can be. But only if you learn the right lessons, and that means being open to taking your share of the blame and above all not looking for scapegoats.

"All the business of war, and indeed all the business of life, is to endeavour to find out what you don't know from what you do; that's what I call 'guessing what was at the other side of the hill'"

The Duke of Wellington.

CHAPTER VI

Was the Dardanelles Campaign Nothing But a Failure, a Waste of Money and Lives, and Are There Lessons For Us All Today?

For many people the Dardanelles Campaign of 1915 is synonymous with failure and is remembered as one of the worst episodes in the First World War. The only question to be asked, if any, is how to apportion the blame. In this article I intend to move beyond that in order to see if there are lessons for us today, in business and in life in general, especially in connection with the management of risk.

The Objective.

By as early as the beginning of 1915 Winston Churchill, The First Lord of the Admiralty, was appalled at the way the War was going, at the apparent stalemate in the trenches on the Western Front and at the acknowledgement that it was becoming a war of attrition. He was frustrated that nobody seemed to have a plan for a breakthrough to achieve an early victory. He devised the plan for a campaign in the Dardanelles as a possible solution. The aim was to capture

Constantinople from Germany's ally the Turkish Empire, and draw a lot of the efforts of our enemies away from the Western Font, or from the Russian Front, or even both.

The Result.

The campaign went on for many months, resulting in a very high loss of life, and was ultimately unsuccessful. Churchill was blamed for proposing the plan in the first place, for many of the specific mistakes, and for continuing with it once it had become obvious to almost everyone else that it was not working, although some people believe it was a good plan but not carried out very well.   This failure led to hid becoming extremely unpopular, and was one factor in his being dropped from the Government for over a year.

Different historians have different views as to the main reasons for this failure. The list includes:

- Poor planning,
- Underestimating the problems,
- Beginning too soon, before everything was ready,
- Using civilian mine-sweepers, rather than servicemen,
- Giving the enemy time to get reinforcements and strengthen the defences,

- Lack of commitment by some of the commanders,
- Poor communication between the Army and Navy.

To sum this up, it is thought of as a good example of "How Not to Do It".

What If...

There has been far less discussion of what might have been, if it had succeeded. Now I know that whenever you say "if only" someone says you need to forget that and concentrate on dealing with things as they are, and usually that is good advice, but just for once I would like us to dwell on "if only" a little. Think about the effects on the World if:

- The War had ended two years earlier than it did.
- Britain had not been taken to the edge of starvation.
- Germany had not been devastated. (Would the Kaiser have survived?)
- Russia had not endured such losses – would the Revolution have happened?
- America had not needed to join the War.
- Women had not been needed to work in factories.

One thing is almost certain. Both Churchill and Prime Minister Asquith would have been a lot more popular. Would Lloyd George have become Prime Minister?

Was It Just a Gamble?

You could say that Churchill took a gamble and lost. But that is not quite fair. There were risks in not doing anything, but allowing the war of attrition to continue. The difference between gambling and Risk Management is that in gambling no risk exists unless you choose to accept it. Risk Management attempts to manage those risks which already exist. I am unaffected by the outcome of the Derby, the Grand National, the F.A. Cup, the Test Match, or the Boat Race, unless I choose to place a bet, whereas the risks in my business are there whether I like it or not. I remember a cartoon in one of the daily papers back in the 1970's. It showed two businessmen passing a news-stand. There were two posters beside it. One read "Ali to fight Frazier" whilst the other read "Heath to fight inflation". One of the businessmen comments "at least with Ali and Frazier we can choose which one to back." He obviously recognised that we all had a vested interest in the battle with inflation. Doing nothing is not necessarily the safe option. Some businesses have gone out of business because they failed to take a chance.

So when things go wrong it is always good to ask "Why?" but it also worth asking what your other options had been and what were the potential risks with each of those.

The Dardanelles Campaign was certainly a failure, but I am not so sure it was a mistake, given the options, and the opportunities.

"It is the customary fate of new truths to begin as heresies and end as superstitions."

T.H.Huxley.

CHAPTER VII

If You Think Risk Management Is Common Sense, See How That Nearly Lost Us The War In 1917.

At a time of possibly the greatest ever threat to Britain's survival, a well-thought-out solution was strongly opposed by many, because it appeared obvious that it would increase rather than reduce the risk. Fortunately the right view finally prevailed and was soon vindicated by events.

The Danger.

In early 1917, after over two years of war, the worst risk Britain faced was not defeat on the battlefield, but starvation. German submarines were successfully attacking merchant ships bringing food from the Americas and West Africa. Over 600,000 tons of shipping were being lost every month. It is estimated that there was enough food in the country to last only six weeks.

What Was The Solution?

The plan proposed by the Cabinet led by Prime Minister David Lloyd-George, in March 1917, was to adopt a convoy system similar to those operated successfully on the shorter routes across the Channel and the North Sea. The idea was to send up to twenty merchant ships together with an escort from the Royal Navy, rather than letting them spread out, taking different routes.

The Opposition.

There were a number of objections to the plan, many raising practical issues, which I will not go into. The most important objection, however, was of a theoretical nature. The concern was that twenty ships spread out all over the Atlantic Ocean would be harder for the enemy to find than if they were all together, and that an attack could destroy a whole convoy, whilst it was unlikely the Germans would find and sink all the ships if they were travelling separately. The Admiralty, with the support of a lot of merchant captains, rejected the plan until it was imposed on them by the Cabinet in April after over 800,000 tons of shipping were lost in a month.

The Crucial Difference: Scale!

The aspect of the argument overlooked by the objectors was one of scale. If I hid a number of small objects, such as coins, in your office, you would be more likely to find them all if they were all in the same drawer than if I hid each one in a different place. Now imagine they are somewhere in a multi-storey office block and you do not know which room, or even which floor, I have chosen, and you have only a limited time in which to look, as the Germans had. If I put one on each floor, you will have more chance of finding at least one than if they are all together and you were never even warm during your search. There is also the point, when considering the actual problem, that if a submarine managed to sink one ship in a convoy it would be unlikely to hit a second, let alone a third, as the escort ships would use depth charges in response to an attack.

The Amazingly Conclusive Result.

The effectiveness of the convoy system was almost unbelievable: losses were more than halved almost at once, and from May 1917 to the end of the war on 11 November 1918 the Germans managed to sink only 138 ships out of the 16,000 convoyed across the Atlantic.

Why Did So Many People Not Get It?

I do not believe the opponents of the convoy system were stupid or unpatriotic. I would have taken some convincing, as the idea does seem to go against reason until you really study it.

Sometimes common sense is not enough. Sometimes you need to take a hard, objective, scientific look at a problem. Or listen to the experts.

"For want of a nail a shoe was lost;

For want of a shoe a horse was lost;

For want of a horse a rider was lost;

For want of a rider a battle was lot;

For want of a battle a war was lost."

Benjamin Franklin.

CHAPTER VIII

Supplies! Supplies!

Most people tend to assume that wars are won and lost by the soldiers on the battlefield. Of course, the numbers, training, discipline and morale of those men do count for quite a lot. Some might give some of the credit or blame to the generals. There is plenty of evidence that the right tactics and strategy can make all the difference. Far fewer people stop and think about the importance of supplies, or logistics to use a more technical word. Yet many great generals would agree that looking after the apparently mundane aspects of warfare can be far more important than is often imagined. Malborough and Wellington both said so.

In the First World War getting the right supplies to the Front became a crucial issue and was probably one of the decisive factors in the final allied victory. For a long time British Industry struggled to produce and deliver all the bullets, shells and replacement parts for the various guns and tanks in use. It was even difficult to get enough uniforms and everyday items to where they were needed. About half-way through the War, the Ministry of Supply came under the control of David Lloyd George for just long enough for him to appreciate the problems before he became Prime Minister.

At that point he ensured that he was replaced at Supply by someone who would be sufficiently determined and energetic to get things moving, someone who would not be afraid to ruffle a few feathers if necessary (and it was). The man he chose was his old friend Winston Churchill, newly rehabilitated after a period out of office. They got the supply issues sorted out just in time to ensure no British soldiers were inadequately equipped when they had to resist the final big German push of 1918.

In Our Time the same is true. I once heard Norman Schwartzkopf, who commanded the American forces in the First Gulf War in the 1990's, speaking on TV of how big a part logistics played in that campaign. He said that it was useless to have a brilliant plan for defeating your enemy if you had no idea how to get your army to where it needed to be, or if most of your men died of hunger, thirst or disease, before they came anywhere near the enemy.

In Your Business the same is probably also true. Yet many business managers concentrate so much on improving or maintaining the efficiency of their own organisations that they do not have the time to look at their supply chain. This is an increasing problem, as has been reported by the Institute of Risk Management. The most apparent cause is the increased reliance on outsourcing and partnering, which are often desirable practices as long as the inherent risks are properly managed.

- How much impact would an interruption in supply have on your business?
- Do you know how vulnerable your suppliers are to any particular risks?
- How many days' supplies do they carry?
- What measures do they have for dealing with threats to their production or distribution?
- What alternative sources of supply do you have? How available are they?

If you do not have current, satisfactory answers to these questions, it is time for you to review your supply chain and its risks. That could put you ahead of the competition.

"Before this time tomorrow I shall have gained a peerage, or Westminster Abbey."

Admiral Horatio Nelson.

CHAPTER IX

Breakthrough!

Sometimes risks and opportunities are closer than we think. This chapter looks at the way the breakthrough came unexpectedly which led to the end of the First World War because an opportunity was found hiding behind a big risk. Fortunately we took it at the right moment, otherwise the result could have been very different.

The First World War ended quite suddenly and unexpectedly, involving a remarkable turnaround of fortunes. After nearly four years of stalemate nobody was expecting a quick and decisive victory, but that was what happened.

Nearly the End.

In 1917 the Germans had almost succeeded in bringing Britain to the point of starvation by attacking our merchant shipping with their submarines, but the initial success of that strategy did not last due to the introduction of the convoy system which enabled the vast majority of transatlantic voyages to be completed successfully. The stalemate in the trenches of the

Western Front looked set to continue for a very long time, but two other major events took place in that year.

In the West.

The first was the decision of the United States to enter the War on the side of the allies, although it took a long time to translate the decision into reality on the battlefield, but the additional troops did make a difference. This was partly a matter of sheer numbers, but it was possibly even more important in its effects on morale: for the British and our allies it brought encouragement, whilst for the Germans it made victory seem even more remote than before.

In the East.

The second big event was the Russian Revolution. After the Tsar's abdication the Government led by the liberal Alexander Kerensky continued to wage war on Germany, but with no more success. The prospect of peace was one of the factors which made people turn to Lenin, who soon fulfilled that particular promise. In fact he was so determined to bring Russia out of the War that he made almost every concession the Germans asked for.

By 1918, this left Germany free to move a large number of troops from the Eastern Front to reinforce those fighting in the West. The German Field Martial von

Ludendorff tried to make the most of the opportunity and set in motion a campaign to break through the allied lines and push on into France. This created a real sense of emergency in Britain with many more men volunteering for the Army and others working extra hours in mines, steelworks and munitions factories to ensure our troops had adequate supplies.

Why did the German plan fail?

It was on a journey to the Front to check the supply position, that Winston Churchill, then Minister of Supply, discovered the possibility of turning the situation into an allied victory. He heard of it from the French Field Martial Foche, who explained that the Germans were in danger of overstretching themselves and becoming vulnerable to a counter-attack, as long as the British and French did not allow themselves to be totally defeated or demoralised by the likely initial German successes. And that is exactly what happened. The early German successes were soon forgotten as the Allies counter-attacked vigorously and effectively. The Germans were unable to retreat and regroup in time to stop the allied advance which led to a complete victory and an Armistice which amounted to total surrender.

How does that relate to anything in your business or any other part of your life today?

When things look bad, very bad, look for the opportunity to turn the situation around. Perhaps a failure in one thing will give you the opportunity to expand your business in another direction. But you can only do that if you do not let the initial setback push you into despair or panic, or be distracted into looking for someone to blame, even yourself. When there is a storm most birds look for somewhere to perch or go into their nests, but eagles see it as an opportunity to use the strong winds and air currents to fly higher and take advantage of the extra height to look for prey on the ground.

Do you see every problem as a threat to your survival, or do you look beyond it to the opportunities? Risk Management means not only assessing the risks but also seeing the opportunities!

"Nothing except a battle lost can be half so melancholy as a battle won."

The Duke of Wellington.

CHAPTER X

Was Ever a Victory So Little Celebrated?

One of the strangest things about the First World War is that in Britain the fact that we won is scarcely mentioned. The end of that war is usually referred to as the Armistice or simply the End of Hostilities, and Armistice Day is commemorated solemnly with the emphasis almost solely on remembering the dead. Think of the contrast with the activities associated with VE Day both in the immediate reactions in 1945 to the news the war was over, and in subsequent annual celebrations. The same element of celebration of victory seems to have been true at the end of the Napoleonic Wars and many others.

The only other major wars to be remembered without an element of rejoicing are the ones which did not end with a decisive victory, such as the Boer War. In America the Civil War is somewhat unusual in that there were Americans on both sides and there has always been an awareness of the need to be sensitive to the feelings of those who supported the South.

Poetic Injustice?

The reaction to the First World War may owe something to the many writers and poets who during and after that war wrote only of the waste and suffering, generally regarding the whole thing as pointless, and not caring which side won. They were not alone. Even the leaders at the time, notably Prime Minister David Lloyd George, and Field Martial Douglas Haigh, said hardly anything about victory in their memoirs. They concentrated on the sadness they felt and were apologetic about their actions, almost as if we had lost, and few people look back on them, especially Haigh and the other generals, as heroes.

Now let me be quite clear. I do not want to minimise the sufferings and sacrifices made, and elsewhere in this book I have been critical of the way the war was fought, and of the failure to prevent it. The fact that I wish the War could have been prevented does not mean that I regard the outcome as being of no importance. If we had lost, a lot of things would have been very different for the World as well as for Britain. All that effort was not for nothing, and I believe it is unfair on the leaders as well as on the soldiers and civilians who played their part in the victory to fail to give them a certain amount of credit.

Somehow the image of the War being a tragic waste has remained with us.

What Have I Got To Celebrate?

Are there things in your life, either your business or professional life, or your personal life, which you look back on with nothing but regret? I am not saying regret, remorse and guilt are always wrong. They have their place. There is however a time to move beyond them and ask what lessons can be learnt, and also a time to look for the positive things among the negative. Are there not some achievements for you to be proud of even along with the things to be sorry for?

If we only find blame, even self-blame, we will not be able to grow as a result of our experiences, good and bad. So learn the lessons, but see the good as well as the bad, even if other people can do nothing but blame you. It is how you see yourself that matters, at least as much as how others see you.

"There never was a good war

or a bad peace."

Benjamin Franklin.

CHAPTER XI

If We Could Lose the Peace After Winning the War, Are You About to Cause the Very Thing You Most Want to Avoid?

After all the suffering of the First World War, it is hard to imagine anyone wanting another war in just over 20 years of the Armistice. This chapter looks at some of the reasons things went so badly wrong and suggests similarities with mistakes we all too often make in business and in life.

What were the Allies trying to do?

Fear was a major factor in motivating the architects of the Peace of Versailles: fear of another war and fear of Germany. This resulted in very severe terms imposed on Germany. In America there was a strong isolationist movement, just when some active engagement in Europe might have been helpful.

What was happening in Germany?

In Germany, the sense of defeat, aggravated by the harshness of the terms of the Peace, led to a sense of injustice and a desire for revenge. These feelings were made worse by the poverty which afflicted Germany even more than the rest of Europe during the inter-war years, especially after the Wall Street Crash.

Germany was required to pay "Reparations" i.e. a form of collective compensation to the Allies for the damage done by the War, at a time when the German economy could not stand it. The waiving of this requirement by the other nations came too late to prevent the catastrophe which was to follow.

Restrictions were placed by the Treaty on German Rearmament, in order to prevent another war, but these added to the resentment, and later were not enforced just when the country was entering into a new phase of militarism.

So who am I blaming?

Just as the British and other nations adopted policies which contributed towards the very things they were intended to prevent, the Germans drew all the wrong lessons from the War and its aftermath. They blamed all the other counties for the way they were treated, but failed to look at the wrong policies which had caused them to go to war in the first place, and made the Jews and other minorities into scapegoats for the failings of the whole nation.

What did we do when the Nazis took over?

When eventually Naziism arose in Germany, the rest of the World looked the other way, as most people seem to have convinced themselves that it was only a matter for Germany and did not threaten anyone else. When Germany did start attacking other countries, Britain and most other nations responded with a policy of "Appeasement," which had the opposite effect to that intended. Instead of being satisfied with moderate gains, Hitler took this as encouragement to be ever more daring.

What about us? Now?

Do you see parallels between these events and things which happen in your life and especially in your business?

Do you ever introduce policies to prevent something undesirable, only to find that these very policies contribute to it? We all are guilty at times of overreacting to problems and at other times of underreacting. We can certainly waste money on ineffective solutions.

Many people get a bad impression of Risk Management because they encounter controls which are unnecessary and ineffective. Sadly, if you have worked in an organisation where managers adopt control measures mainly because they make them appear to be doing something, rather than for their effectiveness, you will have gained the impression that Risk Management is a waste of time and resources, and you will probably have become frustrated and disillusioned too.

Risk Management is badly served by managers who create excessive controls, especially if they are ineffective.

This reminds me of the rhinoceros, which has a horn, supposedly to defend itself. In fact the rhino's worst enemies are poachers who want the horn for its high value due to its imaginary medicinal properties. So as a defence it is worse than useless, like a lot of risk control measures. Or like the cowboy who wore two guns in case he missed six times and was still alive!

Controls Which Do Not Control Anything.

I have often come across this kind of "thinking".

- Money Bags. Carrying cash in a box or bag obviously made for the purpose acts as an advert to thieves, but remains a popular choice.
- Matting Under Climbing Frames. The better the landing surface, the more daring the children will be, and the more injuries will occur, and the more likely it is that parents will blame the owners of the facility.
- IT Controls. Many "controls" in IT departments serve only to shift blame between teams, creating complacency and doing nothing to reduce errors.
- Superfluous Audit Checks. Sometimes the most time-consuming checks are the least effective (let alone cost-effective) as only honest people comply, whilst fraudsters can easily get round them.
- Inspection Systems. If not backed up with rapid repair responses, these can simply prove that you were aware of the defect and thus liable!
- Right to the top. There were lots of regulations in place which were of no real help in the Banking Crisis and in the Horsemeat Scandal. Will they be replaced by anything better? Or only more bureaucracy?

Balance is not always easy to achieve and it is often harder when we are too close to a problem. An independent view, either from within your organisation or from outside, can be a big help. Anyway, do try to review your risks and your control measures frequently and thoroughly.

"Diseases desperate grown, by desperate appliance are relieved, or not at all."

William Shakespeare, Hamlet.

CHAPTER XII

Don't Panic It's Only 'Flu!

You may have heard of the Spanish 'Flu pandemic of 1919. Well I thought I knew a little about it, and therefore thought I knew more than a lot of people. I have recently discovered, however, that what little I thought I knew was largely wrong! While in the process of correcting my misconceptions, I reflected on a number of questions the story raised in my mind, and drew some lessons to apply in business and everyday life.

What's Its Name?

The first thing I had to correct was the name: it was not Spanish, and it did not begin in 1919. It began in January 1918, or possibly a little earlier, and continued until December 1920. Experts disagree as to the place where it originated. Candidates include China, America and Canada. Spain is not one of them, but was the most publicised country to be affected, partly because the story was given particular prominence in the Spanish press because one of the disease's victims, who eventually recovered, was the King, and being neutral in the Great War, it was one of the few countries not subject to severe press censorship.

Keep It Quiet!

In other countries reporting the extent and seriousness of the 'flu pandemic was "discouraged" because the authorities feared that it would be a further blow to morale, but they permitted the publication of this and other stories about events in neutral countries. The British press did not exactly cover up the seriousness of the pandemic at home, but they did not give it much prominence, nor whip up panic, with doom-filled predictions, in the way much less serious epidemics have been reported in recent years.

What Has The War Got To Do With It?

There is considerable disagreement as to the relationship between the pandemic and the War. It is clear that the War did not directly cause the disease, but it may have contributed to its spread. The number of people moving long distances may have helped the disease to travel. The weakening effects of living in such harsh conditions may have made soldiers and civilians more susceptible to the disease.

On the other hand, there is evidence that this particular form of 'flu was more deadly for healthy young people than for older or younger ones. Death seems to have been caused by an over-reaction of the body's immune system. So the weakening effects of the wartime economy may not have played much part in it. It is also likely that soldiers received better medical treatment than most civilians, in the days before the NHS. It is also important to note that the disease affected many parts of the World not involved in the War, such as Indonesia, Africa, and South America.

This is a warning against making easy assumptions about cause and effect in any situation. It is especially important in making good decisions in management, including managing risks. We need to go beyond the "facts" and ask "why?" before coming to any conclusions.

How Bad Was It?

The numbers are almost unbelievable, whether you take the highest or lowest estimates. In three years 500 million people were infected, about a third of the world's population at the time, of whom somewhere between 50 million and 100 million died, or about 4 percent of the world's population, and a particularly high proportion of those infected, 20%. It was probably worse than the Black Death. In Britain "only" about 250,000 died. In the U.S.A. the pandemic affected about two or three million people of whom from 500,000 to 700,000 died.

The numbers of servicemen killed on both sides in the First World War are probably around nine or ten million and probably a similar number of civilians died as a result of the war, from various causes, including starvation and various diseases, apart from the 'flu. In Britain the numbers are around 700,000 to 900,000 servicemen, and probably another 100,000 civilians. It is therefore perhaps understandable that in Britain the War is remembered far more than the 'flu pandemic. On a worldwide scale, however, it can be seen that the pandemic was a far greater catastrophe than the War. In the U.S.A. the War accounted for the deaths of around 100,000 servicemen and a similar number of civilians: a much smaller number than those who died of the 'flu.

Yet it is the War that has had the attention of historians, politicians, artists, poets, and writers of all kinds, in most countries. I have never heard a poem about the 'flu.

Questions.

Now of course, it was, and is, right to ask "Why". It is also worthwhile to try to learn lessons, to hope to prevent another War, to see if the numbers of casualties could have been fewer, to think of better ways of treating the physical and mental wounds incurred by so many. We should of course remember those who gave their lives in that conflict. Let us never forget.

Were there not lessons to be learned from the 'flu pandemic too? Could we have stopped it before it reached such huge proportions? Could our response have been better managed, to reduce the number of deaths and to mitigate its effect on the economy? You may reply that the medical profession did study the pandemic and produce reports and theses on the issues raised, and that eventually, governments did respond.

I would say that the political and social response was at least as inadequate as the efforts at preventing further wars. I remember the ineptitude with which the 2001 Foot and Mouth epidemic was handled by the authorities, as if nobody had learnt anything since 1919. Fortunately that disease only affects animals.

What Is Your Reaction?

Did the public accept the pandemic as beyond anyone's control? Otherwise, why were there not the same sorts of protests demanding "Never again!" as there were against militarisation in many countries in the inter-war years, and subsequently? I believe that this shows how our perception of an event, and therefore our reaction to it, can be influenced by the way it is reported. Who sets the agenda?

I know, from many years of handling liability claims, that what happens after an accident can be as important as what did or did not happen in the first place. Attempted denials, blaming the victim, a casual attitude to your responsibilities, a lack of sympathy for a victim, or a premature admission can all do serious damage to your reputation, whether the accident was your fault or not, whilst sometimes a cover-up can do more harm to an organisation's reputation than the facts which they sought to cover up.

So not only do we need to be careful how we interpret the News, but we also need to think how our own deeds and words may be reported. The public's reaction to a mistake we make may be greatly out of proportion to the actual seriousness of the event.

"This is not the end.

It is not even the beginning of the end.

It is perhaps the end of the beginning."

Winston Churchill.

And Finally.

I hope you have discovered at least something in the preceding pages that you find helpful as well as interesting or amusing. History should not be relegated to museums and libraries, but should be made to work for us, living in the present. In this way it can be re-examined by each generation and new meanings and interpretations can be discovered. In at least this one way the First World War might not have been a complete waste.

If some people disagree with certain of my interpretations of the events of the period, I will not be too concerned. That is not only because I am I not writing for academic historians, but also because if I cause people to challenge my views I am also causing them to challenge their own, and who knows where that may lead.

Above all I hope I have made you think, so that you will be able to learn lessons too from your own failures, and even from your successes, as well as from everyone else's. If I have done that, then through this book I will have achieved something worthwhile.

JOHN HARVEY MURRAY

After studying Economics and Accountancy at Bristol University, John worked in accountancy and audit in several types of local authority prior to becoming Insurance Officer at St Helens Council where he achieved considerable savings in the cost of insurance and risk, which results compared favourably with those of other authorities, according to independent sources, resulting in an overall cost of risk and insurance some 15% below the average for comparable authorities. This was achieved by improving claims-handling and risk management as well as by restructuring the insurance programme. John also made changes to the Council's insurance tendering process in order to obtain the best value for the money spent on premiums.

He is currently self-employed as JHM Risk Management Services, offering risk management and liability claims-handling services to businesses and other organisations, to enable owners and managers to save time and stress as well as money. He is a member of the accountancy body CIPFA.

Go to www.jhmriskmanagementservices.co.uk

John also writes detective fiction.
Go to www.johnharveymurray.co.uk
Or http://twitter.com/JohnHMurray1

Other Books by John Harvey Murray

Available on Kindle, as paperbacks or e-books

How to Avoid Being Misled by Statistics
Don't be one of the 60% who are below average
https://www.amazon.co.uk/How-Avoid-Being-Misled-Statistics-ebook/dp/B00LPG8VUE

Load the Dice
A guide to managing risks in a small business
https://www.amazon.com/Load-Dice-John-Murray-ebook/dp/B00R58W9NQ

How to Cope with the Church
Practical advice for would-be Christians
https://www.amazon.co.uk/How-cope-Church-John-Murray-ebook/dp/B01LZ53GBS

Fiction:
Accounting for Murder: Double Entry
https://www.amazon.co.uk/Accounting-Murder-Double-Entry-1/dp/1544670990/ref=sr_1_cc_1?s=aps&ie=UTF8&qid=1494098077&sr=1-1-catcorr&keywords=john+harvey+murray

www.ingramcontent.com/pod-product-compliance
Lightning Source LLC
Chambersburg PA
CBHW051334170526
45166CB00002B/807